MINIBEASTS

by Emilie Dufresne

Minneapolis, Minnesota

Credits:
Front Cover –Irin K, Nikolay Antonov, Kuttelvaserova, Purinoi, 4&5 – Sergey Novikov, sandsun, 6&7 – Odua Images, Aleksandra Suzi, 8&9 – Phovoir, Altrendo Images, 10&11 – avtk, Antonio_22, 12&13 – Szczepan Klejbuk, Gregory Johnston, Henrik Larsson, 14&15 – Flower Mariya, Andrew Joseph Folts, Tanpimon Paksai, 16&17 – Oksana Shufrych, Konov, Dmitro Derevyanko, Kuttelvaserova Stuchelova, Nikolay Antonov, 18&19 – Jacob Lund, SewCream, 20&21 – MaskaRad, akepong srichaichana, Ihor Hvozdetskyi, nieriss, Weerayuth, XiXinXing, Ami Parikh. Images are courtesy of Shutterstock.com. With thanks to Getty Images, Thinkstock Photo, and iStockphoto.

Library of Congress Cataloging-in-Publication Data is available at www.loc.gov or upon request from the publisher.

ISBN: 978-1-63691-464-0 (hardcover)
ISBN: 978-1-63691-471-8 (paperback)
ISBN: 978-1-63691-478-7 (ebook)

© 2022 Booklife Publishing
This edition is published by arrangement with Booklife Publishing.

North American adaptations © 2022 Bearport Publishing Company. All rights reserved. No part of this publication may be reproduced in whole or in part, stored in any retrieval system, or transmitted in any form or by any means, electronic, mechanical, photocopying, recording, or otherwise, without written permission from the publisher.

For more information, write to Bearport Publishing, 5357 Penn Avenue South, Minneapolis, MN 55419. Printed in the United States of America.

CONTENTS

Welcome to the Forest 4

Taking Care of Nature 6

Itty-Bitty Forest Friends 8

Different Beasts 10

Under Rocks 12

Hiding in Wood 14

Getting Muddy 16

Up Close 18

Get Making! 20

Time to Think 22

Glossary 24

Index 24

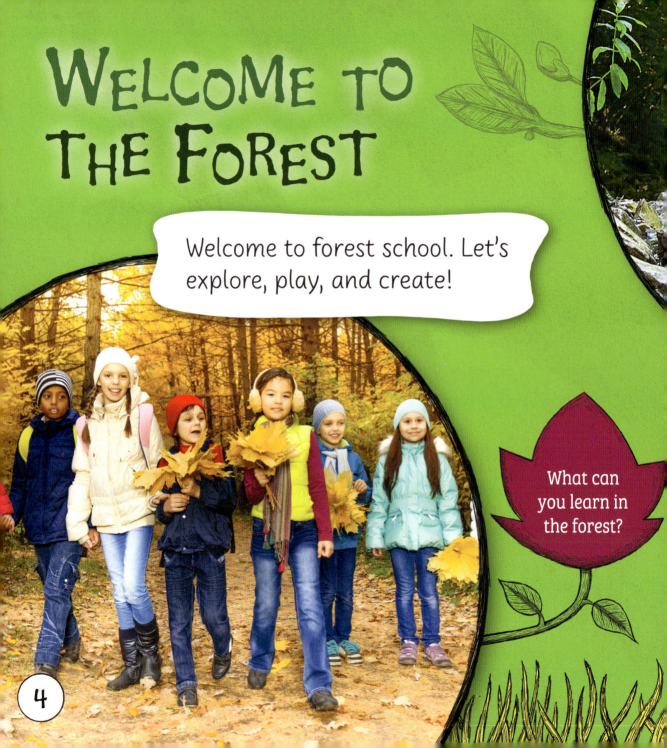

Welcome to the Forest

Welcome to forest school. Let's explore, play, and create!

What can you learn in the forest?

Get ready for forest fun!

We can learn so much from the world around us. Step outside into a great big classroom full of plants, animals, and creepy crawlies.

Taking Care of Nature

Any time we go into **nature**, we should be sure to take care of it. It is important to leave the forest as we found it.

Many plants and animals live in the forest.

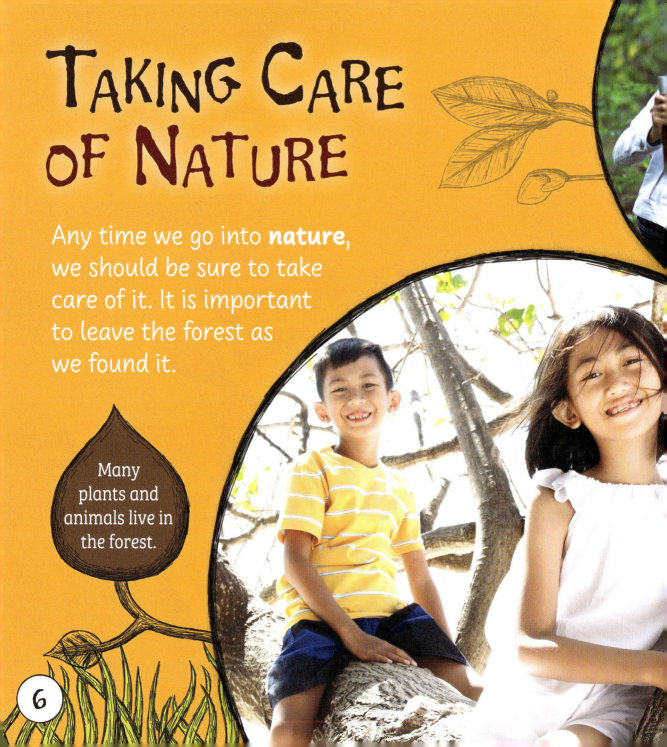

Itty-Bitty Forest Friends

The forest is full of many **creatures**. They are big and small. Let's learn about some of the smallest!

Look carefully to spot tiny creatures.

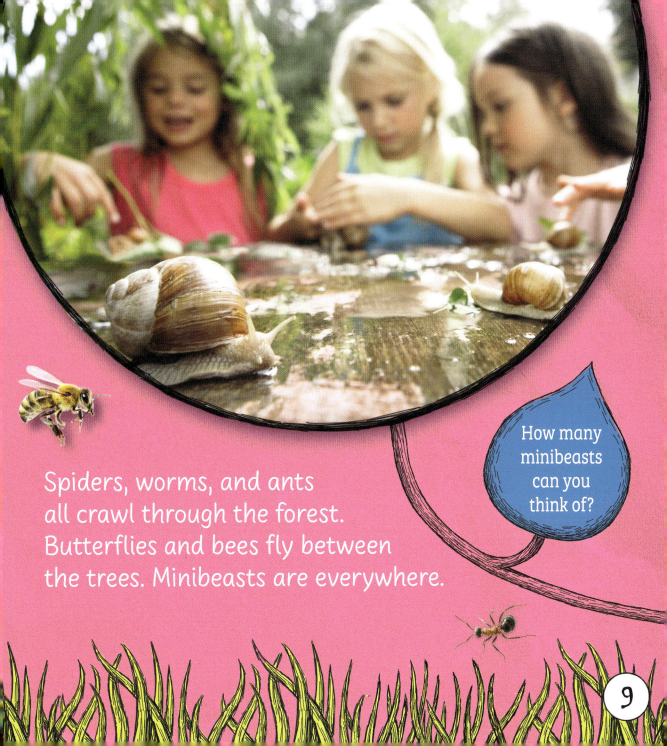

Spiders, worms, and ants all crawl through the forest. Butterflies and bees fly between the trees. Minibeasts are everywhere.

How many minibeasts can you think of?

Minibeasts live in different places. Some make webs. Others live in holes. We can find them on trees and logs or even on the ground.

If you could be a minibeast, which one would you be and where would you live?

Under Rocks

Lots of minibeasts hide on the forest floor. It is often **damp** and dark. Look under rocks to see what might be hiding there. . . .

How do you think the damp forest floor feels? Soft or hard? Warm or cold?

Look at all those pill bugs!

Pill bugs

These minibeasts breathe through **gills** like fish! Their gills need a little bit of water to work best. They can get it from the damp ground.

When you have finished watching, put the rocks back where you found them.

13

Hiding in Wood

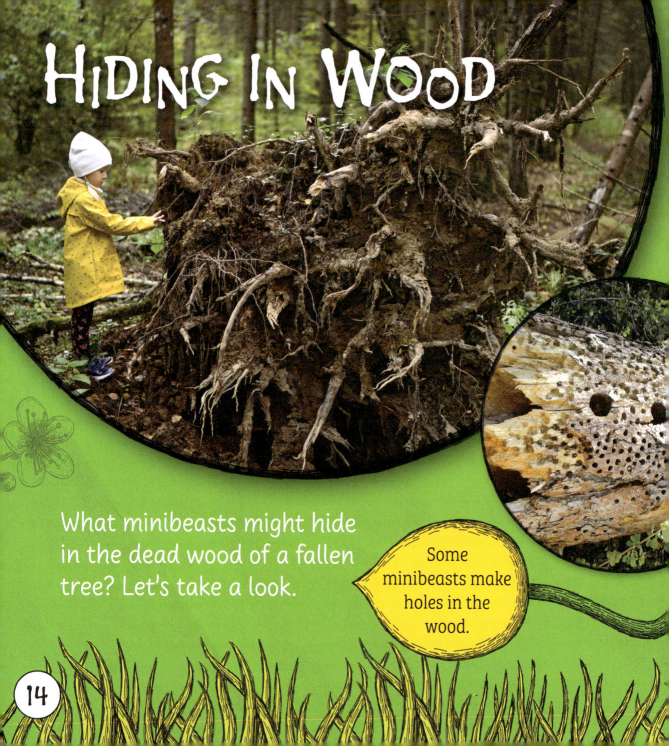

What minibeasts might hide in the dead wood of a fallen tree? Let's take a look.

Some minibeasts make holes in the wood.

Getting Muddy

Some minibeasts live down deep. What can we find if we dig into the dirt?

Ants, **grubs**, and worms can all be found underground!

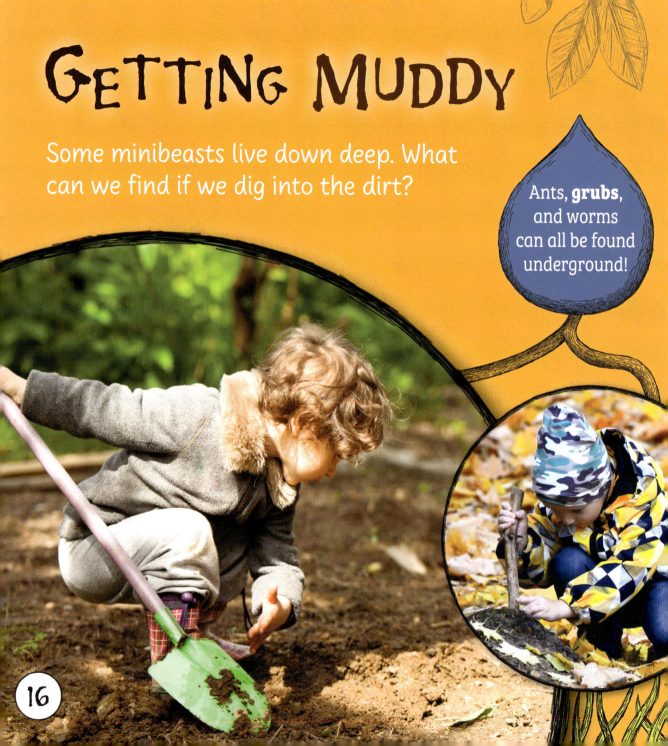

Up Close

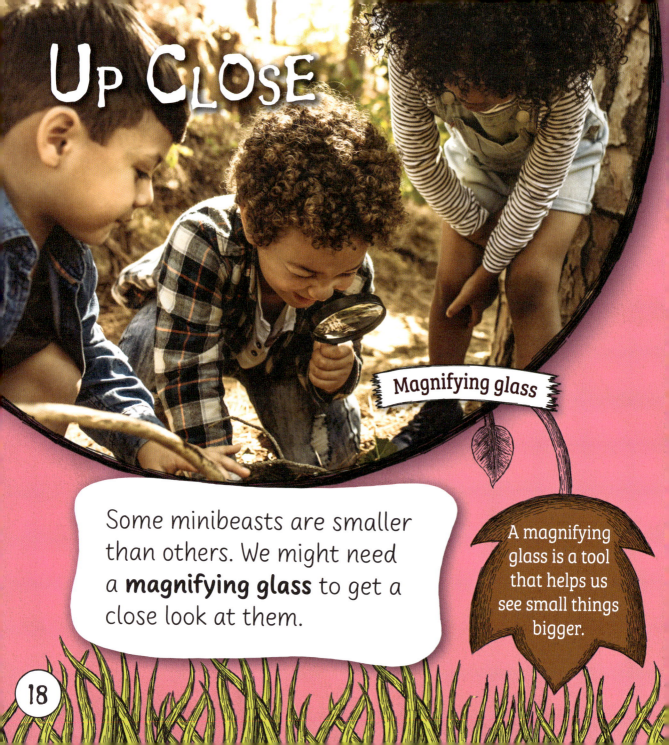

Magnifying glass

Some minibeasts are smaller than others. We might need a **magnifying glass** to get a close look at them.

A magnifying glass is a tool that helps us see small things bigger.

It's easier to look up close at minibeasts that are slower. Speedy ones might crawl away before we can get our magnifying glasses.

Snails are slow. We have lots of time to look at them.

Snail

Get Making!

Have the many kinds of minibeasts sparked your **creativity**? Let's try making something in nature.

What have the minibeasts you've seen looked like? Use things from nature to make a mini mask inspired by minibeasts.

Minibeast mask

Be sure to use only things that have already fallen to the ground.

Want to start a bigger project? Why not try making a minibeast motel. Remember what you learned!

Make different types of spaces for minibeasts to call home.

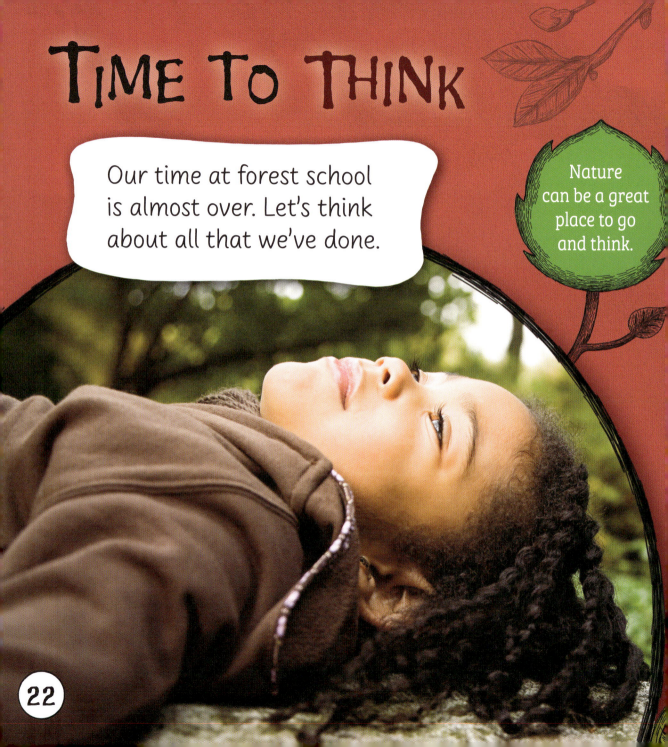

TIME TO THINK

Our time at forest school is almost over. Let's think about all that we've done.

Nature can be a great place to go and think.

GLOSSARY

creativity the ability to imagine, make new things, or think new thoughts

creatures animals, often small in size

damp slightly wet

gills body parts that help animals breathe with water

grubs the young version of minibeasts such as beetles

litter things that have been thrown on the ground

magnifying glass a specially shaped piece of glass with a handle that is used to make objects look larger

nature the world and everything in it that is not made by people

tunnels passages under the ground

INDEX

ants 9, 16–17
forest floor 12
grubs 16–17
magnifying glass 18–19
millipedes 15
pill bugs 13
snails 19
underground 16
wood 14
worms 9, 16–17